CW00881571

How Does an Almond Seed Grow into a Tree.

Yvonne Chan
and Emily Krier

LifeRich Publishing is a registered trademark of The Reader's Digest Association, Inc.

LifeRich Publishing books may be ordered through booksellers or by contacting:

LifeRich Publishing
1663 Liberty Drive
Bloomington, IN 47403
www.liferichpublishing.com
844-686-9607

ISBN: 978-1-4897-3682-6 (sc)
ISBN: 978-1-4897-3681-9 (hc)
ISBN: 978-1-4897-3683-3 (e)

Print information available on the last page.

LifeRich Publishing rev. date: 06/24/2021

How Does an Almond Seed Grow into a Tree.

Yvonne Chan and Emily Krier

To my Heavenly Father,
Almighty God who made the Heavens and the Earth
with such love, wisdom, beauty, and purpose

To my beautiful mama, Linda Chin-Fatt,
whose love, wisdom, and love of Jesus I treasure

And to all my children and grandchildren,
my abundant blessings from the Lord

The cousins Emily, Andrew, Luke, Jonah, Sophia, Anna, John, Abigail, and Clara are in Palo Alto, California, visiting their cousins Charles and Henry. Jonah and Anna have brought their beautiful and excited corgis, Roger and Leena.

ANNA, screaming. Leena, Roger, come back!

JOHN, shouting. They're chasing a squirrel!

JONAH, screaming. Come back!

All the kids are sprinting after the dogs. Roger and Leena are so fast the kids can't keep up.

JONAH: I don't see them! Did anyone see where they went?

ABIGAIL: Oh no! what should we do?

SOPHIA: It's OK, Abby, we'll find them. I think I hear barking.

LUKE: Let's spread out. You guys go that way. You guys go up that way, and we will go this way.

Henry and Clara are running too, but they can't run as fast as the older kids.

EMILY: I'll follow with Henry and Clara.

ANDREW, shouting. I hear them! Look, they're over there, at that tree! The one with the flowers.

JOHN: Oh good, we found them.

The squirrel has run up the tree, and Leena and Roger are barking at it.

CHARLES: Quick, put on their leashes or we could get in trouble. This is Heritage Park, and all dogs have to be on leashes.

Emily, Henry, and Clara finally arrive, panting from the run.

ANNA. Thank you, guys, for helping us find Roger and Leena.

JONAH. Yea, thanks so much.

CLARA. The flowers are so beautiful!

HENRY. This is an almond tree.

They all look up at the beautiful almond tree covered in lovely light-pink blossoms. It is a bright, warm sunny day. There is a very light breeze, and there are some almond flowers on the ground. Roger and Leena are barking and pulling and tugging at their leashes.

ANDREW: Oh, I love almonds. Did you know that you can grow a huge almond tree from a little almond seed?

CHARLES: That's cool! We should try it. I want to know how a small almond seed can grow into a big almond tree.

Henry, interrupted loudly: Hey guys, hurry up, remember Mom is making almond bars! Let's go! Let's go!

They are all running. Roger and Leena are running ahead, pulling Jonah and Anna. They quickly arrive to the wonderful smell of something yummy baking and a chorus of "mmm smells good!"

HENRY: Mmm. I love almonds.

CHARLES: It's not ready. Let's go in the play room. I still want to know how an almond seed can grow into a tree.

ANDREW: Well, Charles the almond nut is like an engine. It has different parts that do different things. Look, Jonah has a picture.

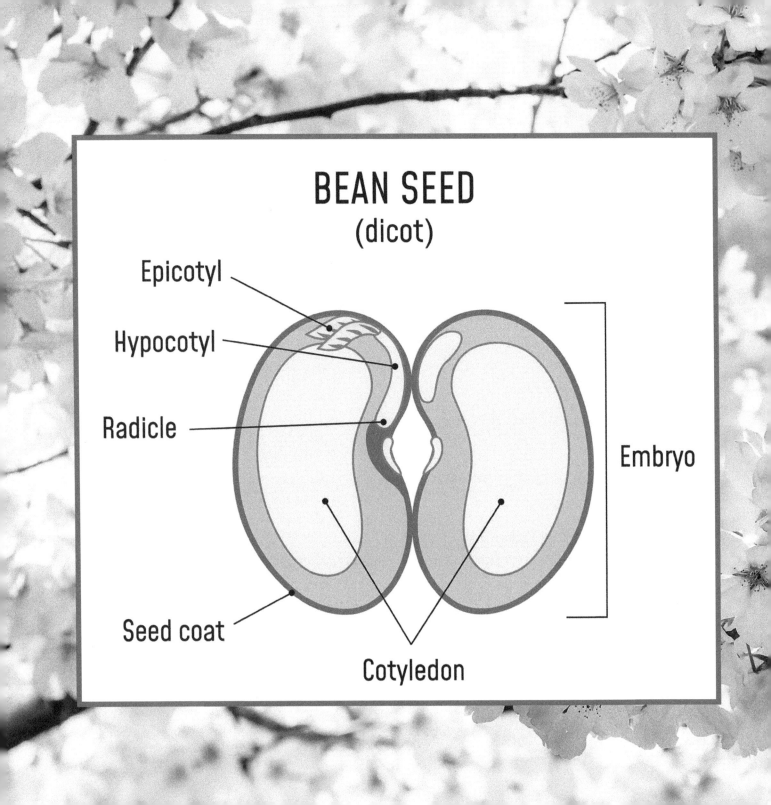

BEAN SEED
(dicot)

Epicotyl

Hypocotyl

Radicle

Seed coat

Cotyledon

Embryo

JONAH: The almond seed has two seed leaves called cotyledons. Inside the seed are other parts with funny names, like embryo, endosperm, and seed coat. The embryo is the part that will grow stems, leaves, and roots that eventually become a big tree. The endosperm is around the embryo and will be food for the baby plant, and the seed coat will protect the baby plant from insects.

JOHN. But how does the seed know what to do?

LUKE. It has something called DNA in its cells, which is like computer code that makes it grow into a tree.

HENRY. Like me! I have DNA.

CLARA. What makes the tree get so big and strong?

LUKE. Photosynthesis. It's like magic.

CLARA. What is photosynthesis?

JONAH. The tree uses light from the sun to make its food.

John. That really does sound like magic. Can you explain?

EMILY. See how the leaves are green? The leaves have something called chlorophyll that makes it green. Chlorophyll takes the energy from sunlight. Trees and plants suck up water through their roots and take carbon dioxide, CO_2, from the air. All together they make food for trees to grow big and strong and bear fruit and release oxygen for us to breathe. It is a very important process because all living things need plants for food and oxygen to breathe.

HENRY. Wow, how did the tree know to do that? Who made it that way?

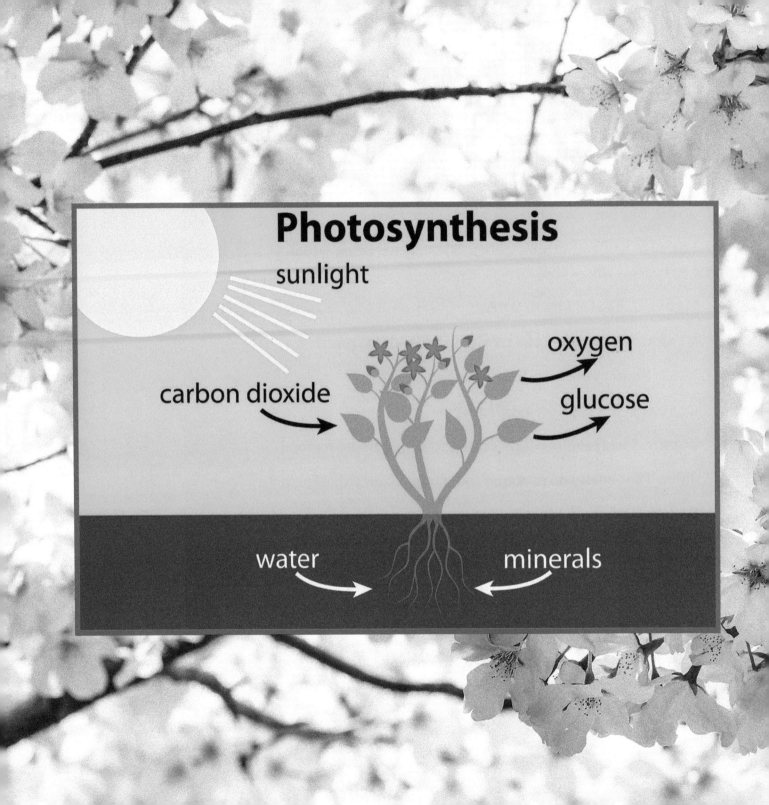

Photosynthesis

sunlight

carbon dioxide

oxygen

glucose

water

minerals

ANNA. Whoa, look at the almond flowers. They're so beautiful. They look like apple blossoms.

CHARLES: How does an almond tree make almonds?

ANNA: Here in California in February and March, the almond tree makes these beautiful flowers. Each flower has many different parts with weird names like *stamen, pistil, stigma, style,* and *ovary.*

EMILY: The almond tree needs honeybees to pollinate the flowers, which then grow into the almond fruit with the seed inside.

ANNA: See how beautiful the almond flowers are? The honeybees also find them beautiful. The flowers also have sweet nectar that bees collect to make honey. That is how they pollinate the flowers.

ABIGAIL: What do you mean, pollinate?

SOPHIA: Honeybees must go from flower to flower to collect nectar and pollen for their food. The flowers need pollen from other flowers to make the fruit. So when a bee goes to a flower, it must get very close to suck up the nectar. The pollen sticks to the hairs on the bee's body, so that when the bee goes to another flower, some of the pollen is transferred to the parts of the flower as needed for pollination.

ABIGAIL: That's interesting! How does the pollen go into the flower?

SOPHIA: The bees bring the pollen when they come to get the sweet nectar. The stigma is very sticky, so when the bees land on the flower, the pollen sticks to the stigma. A pollen tube grows from the pollen grain through the style and into the ovary. The male gamete inside the pollen grain travels through the pollen tube and joins with the female gamete, the ovule, inside the ovary. The genetic material from the pollen and the ovary join to form an embryo that grows into a fruit with seed.

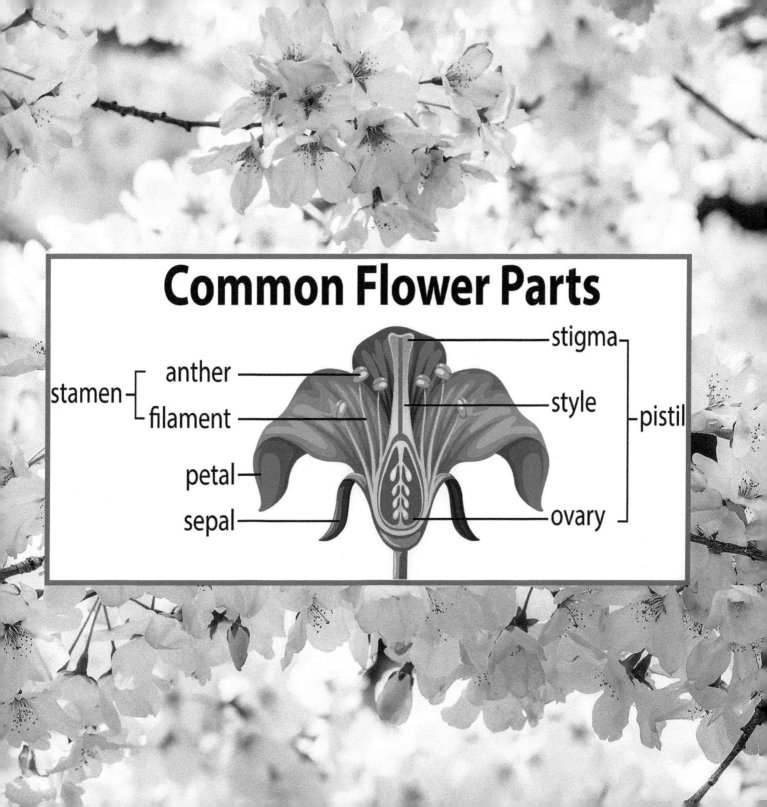

Common Flower Parts

stigma

anther

stamen

filament

style

pistil

petal

sepal

ovary

CHARLES. How did the almond tree and the honeybee learn to do that? It is amazing that they know how to cooperate. The honeybee gets food, and the almond tree gets help to make almonds. That is amazing!

SOPHIA. And the bees make honey for us to eat!

LUKE. That is some awesome computer code in their DNA.

CLARA. I know a song—

(sings)

All things bright and beautiful,
all creatures great and small,
all things wise and wonderful,
the Lord God made them all.

Each little flower that opens,
each little bird that sings,
He made their glowing colors,
He made their tiny wings.

He gave us eyes to see them,
and lips that we might tell,
how great is God Almighty.
Who has made all things well.

ABIGAIL. I know a song too—

(sings)

Jesus loves me this I know,
for the Bible tells me so,

Little ones to Him belong,
they are weak, but He is strong.

Yes, Jesus loves me,
Yes, Jesus loves me,
Yes, Jesus loves me,
for the Bible tells me so.

EMILY: Did you know that Jesus loves everyone, even all the little children?

HENRY. This is so amazing. I want to know more.

ANDREW. Me too! Here's a Bible. Let's look and see what it says:

Then God said, "Let the earth bring forth grass, the herb that yields seed, and the fruit tree that yields fruit according to its kind, whose seed is in itself, on the earth"; and it was so. And the earth brought forth grass, the herb that yields seed according to its kind, and the tree that yields fruit, whose seed is in itself according to its kind. And God saw that it was good. (Genesis 1:11–12 NKJV)

The Lord God planted a garden eastward in Eden, and there He put the man whom He had formed. And out of the ground the Lord God made every tree grow that is pleasant to the sight and good for food. (Genesis 2:8–9 NKJV)

O Lord how manifold are Your works! In wisdom You have made them all. The earth is full of Your possessions. (Psalm 104:24 NKJV)

He has made the earth by His power, He has established the world by His wisdom, and has stretched out the heavens at His discretion. (Jeremiah 10:12 NKJV)

EMILY: When we hurry through our busy days and we come upon precious moments, when we see a beautiful tree, beautiful flowers, or hear birds singing, or see a furry squirrel scampering across our path, little children running and laughing, stop for a moment. Listen, linger a little while, gaze a little bit deeper, smell the flowers, feel God's love for us. Remember the feeling we get when we receive gifts from those we love? We ought to have the same feeling when we come upon the beauty and majesty of nature all around us that God has gifted us.

ANDREW: Our Father in Heaven shows us His love for us in so many, many ways. The beauty and wonder of creation is just one of them. When we see a new born baby, a beautiful sunrise or sunset, a beautiful rainbow in the sky, fresh snow in the trees dazzling like diamonds in the sunlight, beautiful flowers, wild birds and animals and the wonder and joy we feel when we see them are just one way that we experience His love for us. Now we understand His longing for us to love Him in return with all our hearts, with all our souls, with all our strength, and with all our minds.

HENRY: The almond bars are ready! C'mon, let's go eat! Thank you, Mom.

ABIGAIL: Thank you Auntie Christine. The almond bars are so yummy.

Everyone agrees.